Friend.

31 DEVOTIONS PORTRAYING GOD AS FRIEND

NEDRA REID

Introduction

"Revealing the Heart of Christ Through Relationship"

Friendship is one of God's greatest gifts to humanity. From the very beginning, when the Lord walked with Adam in the cool of the day, Scripture unveils a God who initiates and sustains relationships as a means of revealing His covenantal love. We were never intended to traverse life in isolation. In every season, God has ordained that we experience the fullness of life through communion with Him and authentic fellowship with others.

As I reflect upon my own journey, I've experienced the unmistakable hand of God in the friendships He has sovereignly orchestrated. These relationships have affirmed divine gifts, strengthened moral character, inspired purposeful living, and cultivated spiritual maturity. In each relational experience, whether marked by ease or difficulty, the Lord has been revealing more of His heart and His sanctifying purposes.

Yet above all earthly companionships, Christ remains the truest and most faithful friend. Throughout the narrative of Scripture, we see Him walk with sinners, embrace the rejected, and weep with those who mourn. He is the Friend who remains when all others falter. His love is immutable, His mercy unrelenting, and His presence abiding.

This 31-day devotional journey is an invitation to encounter Jesus Christ as your closest and most constant Friend. Each day will immerse you in a biblical narrative, exploring moments where Christ met individuals at the point of their deepest need. We will gain wisdom from friendships that mirror His love and grow in self-awareness through those that expose human frailty.

May this journey draw you closer to the One who calls you friend.

A God sent Friend

This devotional is dedicated to my beloved Uncle Leighton (Pastor Leighton Hugh Palmer), a true embodiment of an intentional and authentic relationship. Our paths crossing was not coincidental but a sovereign intersection, divinely orchestrated within the tapestry of God's perfect will. Through you, Aunt Jo, and the extended Palmer family, I have witnessed God's unwavering desire for deep and meaningful connection.

For almost three decades, our weekly conversations remained a sacred routine, unbroken by geography or the passing of time, a true reflection of intentionality. As I reflect on this journey of kinship and friendship, my heart is overwhelmed with gratitude for the love, wisdom, and dependable presence you so generously shared. Your life was a testament to the power of purposeful relationships, and your legacy continues to echo that truth.

You are my Friend (Excerpt)

Song written, arranged, and recorded by Leighton H. Palmer. 1997

So liberally you gave me all the time I needed. So faithfully, you put your all into the cause. I just want to say how much you mean to me. You are my friend.

You are my friend. You are my friend. I thank the Lord. You are my friend. I thank you, Lord, for sending me someone so special. Thank you, Lord, for sending me someone who listens. Thank you, Lord, for someone special, and she loves me, my niece Nedra. You are my friend.

You are my friend, and I'm truly blessed; yes, I can attest. You are my friend, and I want you to know that I love you so. You are my friend.

Gratitude for your Influence

Thank you, Uncle Leighton, for

Exemplifying a husband's love, devotion, and care for his family.

- Teaching me that true impact comes not from holding multiple church offices but from a deep and personal relationship with Christ.
- Encouraging me to make room for others to grow in their spiritual journey.
- Inspiring me to step beyond my comfort zone in service to God's people, where I've discovered hidden gifts.
- Showing me that human behavior holds profound lessons for those who take the time to discern them.
- Teaching me to drive a manual car while wrecking my nerves with your laughter.
- Emphasizing the necessity of balance in life.
- Showing me that photographs are not just moments captured, but memories cherished.
- And, of course, the unforgettable birthday songs—Christian and Reggae. Your Patois was terrible, but I digress.
- Most importantly, for praying me through.

I am deeply honored and profoundly grateful to have been a *"congregation of one"*, sitting under your wisdom, guidance, and unwavering love. Your honesty, transparency, and intentionality were gifts I never took for granted. Each conversation reflected God's love and care for me. Through your words and actions, you exemplified a faith that was not only preached but lived, one that nurtured, challenged, and inspired. Your presence in my life was a testament to the power of an authentic relationship, and for that, I will always be thankful.

contents

A Friend Who Knows You

"Never will I leave you; never will I forsake you." Hebrews 13:5 (NIV)

The room was filled with whispers. Peter sat in the corner, his face buried in his hands. The weight of his failure pressed against his chest like a crushing stone. He had been forewarned of this occurrence; however, the thought was unfathomable. He had sworn loyalty to Jesus and vowed to stand by His side no matter what. But in the courtyard, under the accusing glare of a servant girl, his courage had failed. Three times, he denied even knowing the man who had called him friend. Now, as the rooster's crow echoed in his memory, shame wrapped around him like a suffocating cloak.

Days passed. Jesus had been crucified, buried, and now, astonishingly, His tomb was empty. Peter had heard the reports, but how could he face Jesus again? He had failed Him when it mattered most. Would Jesus still call him friend? Then came the moment on the shore of Galilee. Weary from a night of fishing, Peter looked toward the shore and saw a figure by the fire. It was Jesus. Instead of condemnation, Jesus asked, "Do you love me?" (John 21:15).

Not once did He remind Peter of his failure. He reassured him of their unbroken friendship and invited him to follow again. In a world where relationships can be shallow and people often fail to see beyond the surface, Jesus offers a profoundly personal friendship. He knew Peter better than he ever knew himself. Psalm 139 reminds us that God has searched and he knows everything about us, even the thoughts we haven't spoken aloud. His knowledge of us is not distant or indifferent, but intimate and compassionate.

How often do we, like Peter, feel unworthy of Christ's friendship? We fail, we fall, and we distance ourselves out of shame. Yet, Jesus never leaves. His friendship is not conditional on our perfection. He does not walk away when we stumble. He remains, waiting to restore, redeem, and remind us that His love is steadfast. No matter where you are today, whether in triumph or regret, Jesus is still by your side, whispering, I will never leave you.

Reflections

- What do you think Jesus sees in you that you struggle to see?
- How does knowing that He never leaves change your perspective on your relationship with Him?

Prayer

Lord, thank You for knowing me better than I know myself. Help me to trust You with every part of my heart, knowing that Your understanding is perfect. Let me grow in my friendship with You, knowing I am fully seen and loved.

A friend who sticks closer than a brother.

Proverbs 18:24

Day 2

A Friend Who Listens

"Before they call I will answer; while they are still speaking I will hear." Isaiah 65:24 (NIV)

The streets were noisy, filled with the chatter of merchants and the shuffling of feet. Yet, above it all, a desperate voice rang out: "Jesus, Son of David, have mercy on me!" (Mark 10:47). The crowd turned to see a blind man, Bartimaeus, shouting relentlessly. Annoyed, they tried to silence him. But he cried out even louder.

Then, everything changed. Jesus stopped. He turned toward Bartimaeus and called him forward. The same crowd that had dismissed him now helped him to his feet. And as he stood before Jesus, the Savior asked, "What do you want me to do for you?" (Mark 10:51). The question seemed almost unnecessary; didn't it seem obvious? But Jesus wasn't just interested in the physical need; He wanted Bartimaeus to voice his heart's desire. "Rabbi, I want to see," he replied. And with a word, Jesus restored his sight.

Jesus took time to listen to those who came to Him. Jesus listens with compassion, patience, and love. He does not rush us, dismiss us, or grow weary of our prayers. Even when words fail, He understands our unspoken cries, and the Holy Spirit intercedes on our behalf (Romans 8:26).

Jesus is not a distant, preoccupied friend. He listens not just to our words but to the cries of our hearts.

He hears our whispered prayers in the night, our silent tears, and our unspoken longings. Even when the world tries to dismiss us, Jesus stops. He turns His full attention to us and asks, "What is it you need?" Today, whatever is on your heart, know that Jesus is listening. He hears you, and He cares.

Reflections

- What unspoken prayers have you been holding in your heart?
- Take time today to share them with Jesus, knowing He is listening.

Prayer

Jesus, thank You for always being there to listen. Help me bring every joy, burden, and question to You, trusting in Your deep care. Teach me to recognize Your voice so that our friendship may deepen each day.

It's never too loud for God to hear. He is never too busy to listen.

A Friend Who Walks with You

"Jesus himself came up and walked along with them; but they were kept from recognizing him." Luke 24:15-16 (NIV)

The road to Emmaus stretched before them, but Cleopas and his companion barely noticed the journey. Their hearts were heavy, and their hopes were shattered. Just days before, they had believed Jesus was the Messiah who would redeem Israel. But now, He was gone, crucified, and buried. They had heard rumors of an empty tomb, but what did it matter? He was dead.

Then, a stranger joined them. He walked beside them, asking about their sorrow. He listened as they spoke and then began to teach. Their hearts burned as He opened the Scriptures to them, explaining the suffering Christ had to endure before entering His glory. And when they finally sat down to eat, their eyes were opened—it was Jesus! But just as they recognized Him, He disappeared.

Jesus is the friend who walks with us, even when we don't recognize His presence. We may feel alone in seasons of grief, confusion, or disappointment, but He is near. He listens to our sorrows, speaks truth into our hearts, and gently leads us back to hope. If you feel lost today, know that Jesus is walking beside you, even when you cannot see Him.

True friendship is more than knowing each other; it is about walking through life together. Jesus isn't merely a distant observer; He invites us to journey with Him. He calls us to follow Him, not as servants who merely obey orders but as friends who share His mission (John 15:15).

Jesus desires to walk with you in the same way. He does not expect you to navigate life alone. Whether you are facing a season of joy or hardship, He is beside you, guiding your steps. But walking with Him requires agreement; it means aligning your life with His will and trusting His lead even when the path is uncertain.

Reflections

- Have there been moments when you only recognized Jesus' presence in hindsight?
- How can you trust that He is walking with you even now?

Prayer

Lord Jesus, I seek to walk alongside You during every phase of my life. Please guide me to follow Your path, even when the way forward is unclear. May my heart remain aligned with Yours so that I may progress in step with You each day.

I will walk among you and be your God, and you shall be my people.

Leviticus 26:12

Day 4

A Friend in Our Darkest Moments

"Even though I walk through the darkest valley, I will fear no evil, for you are with me." Psalm 23:4 (NIV)

The night was darker than any he had known. Sweat dripped from Jesus' forehead like drops of blood as He knelt among the twisted olive trees of Gethsemane. The weight of the world's sin pressed heavily on Him, and His soul was overwhelmed with sorrow. He turned to His closest friends Peter, James, and John, hoping they would keep watch with Him in this moment of agony. But when He looked over, they were asleep.

Alone. That was how it felt. As He prayed, pleading for the cup of suffering to pass, there was no comforting hand on His shoulder, no words of reassurance. His friends had failed Him. Yet, in His darkest hour, Jesus was not truly alone. The Father had not abandoned Him. Strength came from heaven to sustain Him, and He rose from prayer, ready to face the cross.

There are moments in our lives when the weight of sorrow seems unbearable, when friends don't understand, even those closest to us cannot stay awake for our pain. But Jesus is the friend who knows what it means to walk through darkness.

He has experienced our circumstances and remains present with us during our times of suffering. When we feel abandoned, He is present. When we are overwhelmed, He strengthens us. Jesus kneels beside you in the garden of your sorrow, and He will not leave.

Reflections

- Have you ever felt alone in your suffering?
- How does knowing Jesus understand your darkest moments bring you comfort?

Prayer

Lord, thank you for being present in my darkest moments and revealing your all-encompassing presence. Thank you for being a calming presence when I am overwhelmed.

He will be
your light
in your
darkest
hour.

A Friend Who Weeps with You

"Jesus wept." John 11:35 (NIV)

Martha ran to meet Him first, her voice trembling with grief. Lord, if you had been here, my brother would not have died (John 11:21). Mary soon followed, falling at His feet, tears streaming down her face. Lazarus, their beloved brother, was gone.

Jesus knew what He was about to do. He knew that in moments, Lazarus would come out of that tomb alive. Yet, as He looked at Mary and Martha's sorrow, He did something unexpected: He wept. The Son of God, the resurrection and the life, stood among His grieving friends and cried with them.

This is the heart of Jesus. He doesn't dismiss our pain with quick fixes or hollow words. He enters into it. He sits with us in our grief, mourning with us even as He prepares to bring restoration. He is the God of miracles and the friend who holds us when we weep.

Jesus' tender heart provides unparalleled comfort in moments of grief and loss. He does not shy away from our tears; instead, He draws near and offers solace that mends the broken parts of our spirit.

His compassion is evident in every word of encouragement and every gentle touch during times of mourning. Jesus understands that sorrow is part of the human experience and promises to walk you through every tear.

Reflections

- Have you ever considered Jesus a friend who grieves with you?
- How does His compassion bring you comfort?

Prayer

Lord, in my moments of grief, I hold fast to Your promise of comfort. Embrace me in Your loving arms and guide me to find peace in Your steadfast presence.

Tears are a language God understands.

A Friend Who Restores

"He heals the brokenhearted and binds up their wounds." Psalm 147:3 (NIV)

She stood at a distance, watching the others draw water from the well. She understood her place according to societal expectations; better not to join them. The whispers, the side glances, the judgment — she had felt them all before. That's why she came at noon, when the sun was high, when she could avoid the stares. But today was different. A man sat by the well, and as she approached, He did the unthinkable. He spoke to her.

"Will you give me a drink?" (John 4:7).

She hesitated. A Jewish man speaking to a Samaritan woman? It was unheard of. But Jesus wasn't like the others. He saw beyond her past, beyond her shame. He knew about the five husbands, the man she now lived with, and the rejection that had shaped her life. Yet, instead of condemnation, He offered her living water—something no one else ever had—He offered restoration.

Jesus is a friend who doesn't avoid our brokenness; He steps into it. He doesn't see us through the lens of our past mistakes but through the eyes of grace.

Like the woman at the well, we may try to hide our wounds, but Jesus meets us there, offering healing and a new beginning. He sees us, truly sees us, and still calls us beloved.

Forgiveness is the cornerstone of a profound friendship. Jesus' forgiveness reached even those who faltered, offering restoration and hope. His forgiveness was not based on our merit but on His infinite love. Jesus invites you to release any burdens of guilt and accept the liberating grace that only a true friend can offer.

Reflections

- Are there areas of your life where you feel unworthy of Jesus' friendship?
- How can you embrace His restoration today?

Prayer

Jesus, thank You for Your boundless forgiveness. Help me to accept and live in the freedom of Your grace, extending that same forgiveness to those around me.

His restorative power is unfathomable.

A Friend Who Defends

*"Then neither do I condemn you,' Jesus declared. 'Go now
and leave your life of sin." John 8:11 (NIV)*

The dust swirled around her as she knelt on the ground,
surrounded by angry voices. They had caught her in the act of
adultery, dragged her through the streets, and now stood
ready to stone her. The law was clear; she deserved death. But
then, another voice broke through the chaos.

"Let any one of you who is without sin be the first to throw a
stone at her." (John 8:7).

Silence. One by one, the accusers dropped their stones and
walked away. When she finally dared to look up, only one man
remained: Jesus. But He didn't hold a stone. He held mercy.
"Neither do I condemn you," He said gently. "Go and sin no
more."

In this moment, the accused experienced Jesus as the friend
who stands between us and our accusers when the world is
quick to judge. When guilt and shame press in, He speaks
gracefully. He doesn't excuse sin but offers a way forward,
free from condemnation. Whatever past mistakes weigh on
you, know that Jesus is your defender. He does not throw
stones; He extends His hand and lifts you up.

Reflections

- Have you ever felt unworthy of grace?
- How does knowing Jesus defends and forgives you change your perspective?

Prayer

Thank you, Lord, for unmerited grace and favor. Knowing you stand in my defense has given renewed hope and a purpose.

You are my
hiding place
and my
shield; I hope
in your word

Psalms 119:114

A Friend Who Calls Us by Name

"Jesus said to her, 'Mary!' She turned toward him and said to Him, 'Rabboni!' (which is to say, Teacher)." John 20:16 (NKJV)

The garden was still. Morning light filtered through the trees, but Mary Magdalene's world remained dark with grief. She had come to the tomb expecting to anoint Jesus' body, but now even that had been taken from her. The stone was rolled away, and the grave was empty. Someone had stolen Him.

Tears blurred her vision as she turned and saw a man standing there. "Sir, if you have carried him away, tell me where you have put him." (John 20:15).

Then He spoke her name. "Mary".

In that moment, everything changed. The voice was familiar, filled with love and tenderness. It was Him. He was alive! Her sorrow turned to joy in an instant.

Jesus is the friend who calls us by name, knowing us intimately rather than another face in the crowd. In our moments of despair, when we might feel unseen or forgotten, He calls out to us with love, affirming that we truly belong to Him. Today, take a moment to listen for His voice. He is calling your name - listen for His voice.

Reflection

- How does knowing Jesus calls you by name change how you see your relationship with Him?

Prayer
Your comprehensive understanding of my identity and your willingness to acknowledge me by name evokes a deep sense of appreciation. I am thankful that you have recognized my existence and that you continue to address me in such a personal manner.

He knows my
name.
He speaks
my name.

A Friend Who Guides Your Decisions

"Trust in the Lord with all your heart, and lean not on your own understanding; in all your ways acknowledge Him, and He shall direct your paths." Proverbs 3:5-6 (NKJV)

The instructions were clear. Abraham's heart must have shattered at God's command. Isaac was not just his son—he was the fulfillment of God's promise. Yet, without hesitation, Abraham obeyed. He climbed Mount Moriah step by step, trusting that God's voice would never lead him astray.

This story is more than one of obedience; it is about friendship. Abraham was called a friend of God (James 2:23), and true friendship is built on trust. Though the command seemed impossible, Abraham believed God, his friend, would provide. And He did. God stopped Abraham's hand at the last moment and provided a ram for the sacrifice.

Jesus, our greatest friend, guides us in ways we may not always comprehend. He calls us to surrender, to trust Him with what we hold most dear. Yet, He never asks us to walk alone. Just as God provided for Abraham, Jesus walks with us, leading us in every decision, even when the path is uncertain.

Reflections

- How has God guided you before?
- What would it look like to trust Him again?

Prayer

Jesus, my Friend and Guide, inspire me to trust You completely. In moments of confusion, remind me that You are always leading me toward Your perfect plan. Teach me to surrender in faith, confident that You will always provide.

Trust His plan even when you don't understand the path.

A Friend Who Invites Us to Rest

"Come to me, all you who are weary and burdened, and I will give you rest." Matthew 11:28 (NIV)

The crowds gathered in large numbers, seeking healing and yearning for hope. From dawn to dusk, Jesus attended to their needs by healing the sick, instructing the lost, and providing nourishment for the hungry. The disciples had little opportunity to pause for sustenance. The demands placed on them were incessant, and the work appeared boundless. In the midst of this relentless activity, Jesus made an unexpected declaration.

"Come with me by yourselves to a quiet place and get some rest." (Mark 6:31).

They retreated to a solitary place, away from the clamor and crowds. In that moment, a stillness enveloped them.

Jesus recognized the necessity of rest. He understood that even in the realm of ministry, the soul requires restorative periods amid the service of others. His concern extended beyond merely the labor of His disciples; He also prioritized their well-being. This invitation remains relevant to individuals today.

Life can be exhausting. Responsibilities accumulate, concerns burden us, and we often compel ourselves to persist. However, Jesus does not solely summon us to engage in work; He invites us to rest, not merely physical rest, but a deeper repose for the soul. In His presence, one discovers tranquility.

Reflections

- Are you feeling weary today?
- How can you respond to Jesus' invitation to rest in Him?

Prayer

Thank you, Lord, for being my place of solace. I am grateful that you have provided mental, physical, and emotional rest. In you I am renewed.

There is safety in His arms.

Day 11

A Friend Who Uplifts

*"Immediately Jesus reached out his hand and caught him.
'You of little faith,' he said, 'why did you doubt?'"*
Matthew 14:31 (NIV)

The wind howled across the sea as waves crashed against the boat. The disciples strained at the oars, their muscles aching from the fight against the storm. Then, out of the darkness, they saw something, or someone, walking on the water. Fear gripped them. A ghost! they thought.

But then came a familiar voice: "Take courage! It is I. Don't be afraid." (Matthew 14:27).

Peter's heart raced. "Lord, if it's you, tell me to come to you on the water." And Jesus said, "Come."

Peter stepped out, his feet touching the impossible. He walked toward Jesus, eyes fixed on Him. But then the wind roared, the waves rose, and fear took over. He began to sink. "Lord, save me!" he cried.

Immediately, Jesus reached out His hand and caught him.

How often have we stepped out in faith, only to falter when fear and doubt creep in? Yet, Jesus does not allow us to drown. He is always near, ready to lift us when we fall. He doesn't condemn us for our weak faith, He strengthens it. If you feel like you're sinking today, reach for His hand. He won't let go.

Reflections

- What areas of your life require you to trust Jesus more?
- How can you fix your eyes on Him instead of your fears?

Prayer

Thank you, Lord, for breaking my fall. For extending a hand of love, acceptance, and encouragement. May I demonstrate your love to others as I grow in understanding.

Faith over fear.

A Friend Who Shows Us Grace

"For from his fullness we have all received, grace upon grace." John 1:16 (ESV)

The table was set, the meal prepared, but Simon the Pharisee watched in disgust as she entered. She was a sinner, a woman of ill repute. She had no place here. But she didn't care about the stares. Her eyes were only on Jesus.

She knelt behind Him, tears spilling onto His feet. With trembling hands, she wiped them with her hair and anointed Him with expensive perfume. The fragrance filled the room. Simon scoffed, "If this man were a prophet, he would know who is touching him."

Jesus turned to him and spoke of grace, a debt forgiven, love poured out in response. Then He looked at the woman and said, "Your sins are forgiven, your faith has saved you; go in peace." (Luke 7:48,50).

Jesus is a friend of grace. Where others see a sinner, He sees a soul redeemed. He welcomes the broken, the outcast, the ones the world rejects. And He offers the same grace to us, inviting us to leave our shame behind and walk in peace.

Reflections

- Have you ever struggled to accept Jesus' grace?
- How can you extend that same grace to others?

Prayer

Your grace continues to be sufficient for me. Help me to realize this whenever I struggle to understand the depth of your love.

God's grace is immeasurable.

A Friend Who Stands in the Fire

"And the fourth looks like a son of the gods."
Daniel 3:25 (NIV)

The heat was unbearable. Flames roared, consuming everything in their path. Shadrach, Meshach, and Abednego had refused to bow to Nebuchadnezzar's golden image, and now, they faced the furnace.

Bound and thrown into the fire, they should have been consumed instantly. But then, the king's eyes widened in shock. "Did we not throw three men into the fire?" he asked. His advisors nodded. "Then why do I see four men walking around, unharmed? And the fourth looks like a son of the gods!"

Jesus was in the fire with them. He didn't remove them from the trial but stood with them in the midst of it, protecting them.

We all face fiery trials, seasons of testing, pain, and loss. But Jesus does not leave us to face them alone. He walks through the fire with us, and when we come out, we are not burned. If you are in a season of suffering, know this: You are not alone. He is in the fire with you.

Reflection

- How does knowing Jesus is with you in your trials change how you face them?

Prayer

Your protection is profoundly sensed as I journey through life, surrounded by trials that threaten to consume, yet leave me unscathed. My lips sing praises for your immovable shield.

No challenge is too difficult for God to demonstrate His omnipotence.

A Friend Who Washes Our Feet

"Now that I, your Lord and Teacher, have washed your feet, you also should wash one another's feet."
John 13:14 (NIV)

The room was silent as Jesus knelt before them, basin in hand. The disciples watched, stunned, as He removed His outer garment and placed a towel across His leg. The Master, the one they followed and revered, was washing their feet.

Peter recoiled. "Lord, you shall never wash my feet!" But Jesus replied, "Unless I wash you, you have no part with me." (John 13:8).

One by one, He moved from disciple to disciple, even Judas, who would betray Him. He knelt before them, cleansing the dust from their feet, modeling a love that serves.

Jesus is the friend who humbles Himself for us. Though He is Lord, He stoops low, taking on the role of a servant. His love is not prideful or distant, it is intimate, personal, and selfless. And He calls us to do the same.

Reflection

- What areas of pride could be transformed through humble service?

Prayer

Lord, help me to see others as You have seen me. May humility guide my relationships so that they may see you through me.

In humility, He guides us.

A Friend Who Gives His Life

"Greater love has no one than this: to lay down one's life for one's friends." John 15:13 (NIV)

The cross stood tall against the darkened sky. Nails pierced His hands and His feet. Blood dripped down His face from the crown of thorns pressed into His brow. The weight of sin bore down upon Him, your sin, and my sin. And yet, He stayed.

The crowd mocked Him, saying, "If you are the Son of God, come down!" But He did not. He remained, enduring the agony and separation from the Father because love held Him there.

Jesus gave His life for us, not because we deserved it, but because His love is greater than our failures. He is the friend who saw our need and stepped into our place. There is no greater love.

Reflection

- How does Jesus' sacrifice deepen your understanding of His friendship?

Prayer

No greater love have I ever received than the Lord laying down his life for me. Thank you for seeing me through your eyes; I am worthy of being saved.

He gave us the ultimate sacrifice so we could remain in a relationship with him.

A Friend Who Calms Our Storms

*"Then he got up and rebuked the winds and the waves,
and it was completely calm." Matthew 8:26 (NIV)*

The sea churned violently, tossing the small boat like a toy in the storm. The disciples, seasoned fishermen, had faced storms before, but nothing like this. Water filled the boat. They were going to drown.

Frantic, they turned to Jesus. But He was asleep. Asleep? How could He rest while they were perishing?

They shook Him awake. "Lord, save us! We're going to drown!"

Jesus rose, looked at the raging sea, and said three words: "Peace, be still." Instantly, the wind ceased, the waves stilled, and the storm obeyed His voice. The disciples stared in awe.

Life brings storms, unexpected, terrifying, and beyond our control. Fear makes us wonder if Jesus is even aware of our struggle. But He is never absent. He is in the boat with us. And when the time is right, He speaks peace over our chaos. If your life feels like a storm today, remember: Jesus is near and has the power to calm it.

Reflection

- What storm in your life do you need to surrender to Jesus today?

Prayer

Dear Jesus, I have encountered Your presence during my most challenging periods. In moments when I believed that hope was lost, You provided tranquility by calming the tumultuous waters, silencing the winds, and alleviating the downpour. I'm grateful, Lord, you have been my source of reassurance when life becomes overpowering.

He is the
shelter in
our storms.

A Friend Who Welcomes the Outcast

"Daughter, your faith has healed you. Go in peace."
Luke 8:48 (NIV)

For twelve years, she endured chronic hemorrhaging, resulting in significant physical weakness and social isolation. This condition rendered her ceremonially unclean, effectively ostracizing her from societal interactions and support systems.

Upon learning about Jesus, she was compelled by a single thought: if she could merely make contact with the hem of His garment, healing might be within reach.

With determination, she navigated through the thronging crowd despite the judgmental whispers and skeptical gazes directed her way. In a moment of desperate resolve, she succeeded in grazing His garment. Remarkably, her bleeding ceased instantly.

In this pivotal moment, Jesus paused and inquired, "Who touched me?" The nearby disciples expressed confusion, overwhelmed by the multitude pressing against Him, yet Jesus possessed an unmistakable awareness of her contact.

Fearful and trembling, she approached Him, fully prepared for condemnation or rejection for her actions. Instead, He addressed her with warmth, referring to her as "daughter."

Through this interaction, it is evident that Jesus actively seeks to embrace those marginalized by society. He possesses an insightful awareness of individuals overlooked by others and extends an invitation to those burdened by brokenness and feelings of inadequacy. He affirmatively claims them as His own.

Reflections

- Have you ever felt unworthy of Jesus' love?
- How does His compassion change the way you see yourself?

Prayer
I'm renewed by the thought of Jesus reaching out to me even in my rags. I am never too filthy for his open arms. Thank you, Lord, for your welcoming arms and warm smile.

Just one touch transcends societal alienation and fosters a loving relationship with God.

A Friend Who Rejoices with Us

"Rejoice with those who rejoice." Romans 12:15 (NIV)

The wedding feast was characterized by vibrant expressions of joy, with an abundance of laughter, music, and dance. However, in the midst of this festivity, a crisis emerged: the wine supply had been exhausted.

Mary approached Jesus, indicating the situation with the simple statement, "They have no more wine." While this dilemma may not have posed a dire threat to life or health, it represented a significant social embarrassment for the hosts, given the cultural expectations of hospitality at such events.

Rather than dismissing the matter, Jesus chose to intervene. He instructed the servants to fill six large stone jars, traditionally used for ritual purification, with water. Subsequently, through a remarkable act of transformation, He converted the water into high-quality wine without any ostentatious display.

This event marked His first documented miracle and is noteworthy not for its demonstration of power over life and death, but rather for its emphasis on joy and celebration.

This narrative highlights a significant insight: Jesus is not merely an ally in times of distress; He actively engages in our moments of celebration. He finds joy in our milestones and the everyday instances of happiness, reflecting His commitment to being present in all aspects of life. His involvement encourages a deeper understanding of the divine nature, which embraces both the trials and triumphs of human experience.

Reflection

- Do you invite Jesus into your joyful moments, or only in times of need?

Prayer

My joy knows no bounds when it is wrapped in you. I hold to you, knowing you have walked my path and celebrated me as I meet each milestone in you.

He shares in
the
celebration
of each of our
milestones.

A Friend Who Heals Our Brokenness

"He heals the brokenhearted and binds up their wounds."
Psalm 147:3 (NIV)

Standing alone among the tombs, bearing physical scars indicative of his struggles, and exhibiting profound psychological distress. He had been ostracized from society, bound in chains, and forcefully expelled from his home. No one intervened on his behalf; he appeared beyond the possibility of rehabilitation.

However, the arrival of Jesus marked a pivotal moment.

The tormenting demons within the man reacted with vehement cries, recognizing His presence. With a mere command, Jesus instructed them to depart, and in that instant, the man experienced liberation from his afflictions.

When the people arrived, they encountered the man, now clothed and exhibiting clarity of thought, positioned at the feet of Jesus. The individual who had once been deemed irretrievable was reintegrated into a state of wholeness.

Jesus exemplifies a transformative presence, addressing not only the physical ailments but also the profound psychological and emotional wounds that afflict individuals. He possesses the insight to recognize our vulnerabilities and facilitates a process of restoration. Regardless of the constraints that may confine you, be they anxiety, substance dependence, or ingrained shame, He holds the capability to liberate you.

Reflection

- What area of brokenness in your life needs Jesus' healing today?

Prayer

Lord, I am thankful for your restorative hope. You brought peace to my life when I created brokenness. You offered healing for every aspect of my life because I am a new creature in you.

He heals the
brokenhearted
and binds up
their wounds.

Psalms 147:3

A Friend Who Carries Our Burdens

"Cast all your anxiety on him because he cares for you."
1 Peter 5:7 (NIV)

Martha experienced significant distress as guests filled her home, leaving her with numerous tasks to complete. She busily prepared food, served drinks, and ensured that every detail was in order, while her sister, Mary, chose to sit at the feet of Jesus.

Martha's frustration peaked as she exclaimed, "Lord, do You not care that my sister has left me to manage all the responsibilities alone? Please instruct her to assist me!"

Jesus turned to her with love, "Martha, Martha, you are worried and upset about many things, but only one thing is needed." (Luke 10:41-42).

While Martha's desire to serve was valid, she had allowed the associated pressures to overwhelm her. Jesus was not advocating for a standard of perfection but rather offering an invitation to find relief in Him.

This story prompts a reflection on how frequently we mirror Martha's tendencies to over-exert ourselves, assuming burdens that exceed our capabilities. Ultimately, Jesus serves as a supportive ally, encouraging us to relinquish our excess responsibilities and place them at His feet

Reflection

- What worries or responsibilities do you need to surrender to Jesus today?

Prayer

Lord, thank you for inviting me to lay my burdens down so I can fully enjoy the relationship you are cultivating with me. May I be fully aware that the burdens I bear are within your control. Thank you for being my burden bearer.

Cast your burden on the Lord, and He shall sustain you.

Psalms 55:22

A Friend Who Encourages Authenticity

"And Jonathan made a covenant with David because he loved him as himself." – 1 Samuel 18:3 (NIV)

Authenticity in relationships is a valuable yet uncommon quality. Many friendships are predicated on utilitarian aspects such as convenience, social standing, or self-interest. In contrast, genuine friendship, especially one that aligns with ethical principles, requires selflessness, loyalty, and steadfastness. Jonathan and David's friendship was a beautiful example of this kind of authenticity, a bond not based on personal advantage but on love, trust, and divine purpose.

Jonathan, the son of King Saul, had every reason to perceive David as a rival for the throne. By birthright, Jonathan was poised to ascend to the throne. Nevertheless, recognizing God's anointing on David, he relinquished his status and ambition. Jonathan's decision to enter into a covenant with David epitomizes this commitment to authenticity. He symbolically surrendered his royal insignia, including his robe, sword, and armor demonstrating a profound level of trust in the divine plan at play. True friendship, therefore, transcends competition and instead fosters an environment where one can celebrate and support the calling and trajectory of another.

Authentic friendship is often tested in times of adversity. When Saul's jealousy escalates into hatred, Jonathan finds himself positioned between his father and his friend. Nevertheless, he remains steadfast in his loyalty to David, providing warnings of impending danger and advocating for him, even when doing so poses a threat to his own life. True friendship endures and remains uncompromising, particularly in challenging circumstances.

Moreover, one of the most compelling demonstrations of Jonathan's authenticity is his willingness to prioritize divine will over personal ambition. He recognizes that David, not himself, is the anointed king chosen by God. Rather than resisting this truth, Jonathan offers his resolute support to David. In a society where individuals frequently prioritize self-advancement, Jonathan's commitment to selflessness in friendship serves as a significant lesson.

This paradigm of friendship mirrors the nature of the relationship that God extends to humanity. Divine love is not contingent upon what individuals can contribute; rather, it is characterized by sacrifice, covenantal fidelity, and unequivocal commitment. Just as Jonathan remained loyal to David, God remains consistently present in our lives. He stands faithful, protective, and continuously working toward our ultimate good.

Reflections

- Do you have friendships that reflect God's authenticity?
- Are you willing to love selflessly, even when it costs you something?
- May we strive to be the kind of friend Jonathan was, and more importantly, may we recognize that God Himself is the most faithful friend we could ever have.

Prayer

Lord, thank You for being a faithful and authentic friend. Help me to be the kind of friend who loves selflessly, supports others in their calling, and remains steadfast through every season. Teach me to build relationships that reflect Your love. In Jesus' name,

Create in me a clean heart, O God, and renew a right spirit within me.

Psalms 51:10

A Friend Who Teaches Patience

"Let perseverance finish its work so that you may be
mature and complete, not lacking anything."
— James 1:4 (NIV)

The path stretched long, dusty, and devoid of company, save for a solitary figure positioned at its edge, observing intently. Day after day, he maintained his vigil, his gaze fixed on the horizon.

The local residents regarded him as imprudent, while the household staff murmured about his apparent stubbornness to relocate. Yet the patriarch remained immovable in his conviction. His son had departed, squandering his inheritance on extravagant and reckless pursuits. Nevertheless, the father exhibited a profound patience, driven by an enduring love that applied no conditions.

Then, one day, a form emerged on the distant horizon. It was gaunt, worn, and seemingly defeated. But it was unmistakably his son. The father acted instantly, disregarding any notions of dignity or decorum, and closed the distance between them. Without waiting for any words of contrition, he enveloped his son in an embrace.

"Father, I have sinned against heaven and against you...'

The father had already ordered a robe, a ring, and a celebratory feast. His patience had proven effective, and his love had remained enduring.

The son who had previously departed has now returned.

This parable, as conveyed by Jesus, serves not merely as a narrative but as a profound reflection of His essence. He exemplifies the patient companion who awaits our return. When individuals stray, He refrains from pursuing them with condemnation; rather, He stands with open arms, yearning for their reintegration.

In all circumstances, be it during periods of waiting, personal growth, or facing challenges Jesus prompts us to cultivate a trust in His timing. He undertakes the refinement of our character, fostering attributes such as patience and resilience as He navigates us through life's complexities. This divine patience is not a mere absence of action; it represents a dynamic and evolving trust in the belief that every delay serves a significant purpose within the broader context of our spiritual journey.

Reflections

- How has waiting on Jesus taught you patience in your life?
- What practical steps can you take to trust His timing even when difficult?

Prayer

Jesus, thank You for teaching me patience. Help me to trust in Your perfect timing, knowing that every season has a purpose in my journey toward becoming complete in You.

He who is slow to wrath has great understanding, but he who is impulsive exalts folly.

Proverbs 14:29

A Friend Who Challenges You to Forgive

"Be kind and compassionate to one another, forgiving each other, just as in Christ God forgave you."
— Ephesians 4:32 (NIV)

Joseph found himself in the presence of the individuals who had betrayed him, his own brothers, who had cast him into a pit, sold him into slavery, and robbed him of numerous years of his life. At that moment, they bowed before him, entirely unaware of his true identity. He possessed every justification for harboring resentment and pursuing vengeance.

Years had elapsed since that fateful day in Canaan. Joseph had faced considerable adversity, including enslavement, unfounded accusations, and imprisonment. Nevertheless, throughout these tribulations, he maintained his faith, believing that God was with him. He now held the esteemed position of Pharaoh's second-in-command, wielding significant authority that encompassed matters of life and death over those who had wronged him.

When the time for revelation arrived, his brothers were filled with fear, anticipating anger and condemnation. Instead, Joseph expressed profound sorrow. He addressed them with reassurance, stating, "Do not be afraid. Am I in the place of God?

You intended to harm me, but God intended it for good to bring about what is now being accomplished: the salvation of many lives." (Genesis 50:19-20)

Joseph experienced significant suffering due to the cruelty of others; however, he discerned the presence of a higher purpose for his pain. Rather than succumbing to bitterness, he opted for forgiveness. He understood that the desire for vengeance was not his prerogative and recognized that even the most adverse circumstances could be utilized by a greater power for a significant outcome.

In this sense, Jesus invites us to embrace a similar approach to forgiveness. This concept does not entail justifying wrongful actions but rather placing trust in a higher power that transcends our suffering. Retaining resentment serves only to imprison us, while the act of releasing such burdens can facilitate personal liberation. Just as God has shown mercy to humanity through Christ, we are urged to extend similar grace to others, even in instances where it may appear undeserved.

Forgiveness represents a crucial element in nurturing deep and restorative relationships. It is a profound and liberating practice that underscores the notion that clinging to bitterness deprives individuals of tranquility. By adopting this paradigm, one can fundamentally transform their perspective, thereby enabling the development of healthier, more affectionate connections with others.

Reflections

- Are there any grudges or resentments you need to release?
- How might extending forgiveness bring you closer to experiencing the fullness of Jesus' friendship?

Prayer

Lord, thank You for the powerful example of forgiveness through Joseph's life. Help me to release any sense of vindication and forgive others, so that I may experience the freedom and peace from Your love.

"...forgiving each other, just as in Christ God forgave you."

Ephesians 4:32

A Friend Who Invites Growth

"I am the vine; you are the branches. If you remain in me and I in you, you will bear much fruit; apart from me you can do nothing." — John 15:5 (NIV)

The vineyard extended across the hillside, its vines laden with ripening fruit. The vinedresser maneuvered skillfully among them, pruning each branch with expertise. He understood that for the branches to yield the best fruit, they required careful trimming, shaping, and, at times, severe reduction of plant structure.

In this context, Jesus employed a powerful metaphor to convey concepts of spiritual growth to His disciples: "I am the vine; you are the branches." He emphasized that a sustained connection with Him would yield abundant fruit. However, the principle of growth inherently involves a process of pruning. There are times when God strategically removes barriers to our development, habits, anxieties, and distractions that impede our potential. Although this process may induce discomfort, it serves a constructive purpose; it is an invitation to deeper growth.

As a guiding figure, Jesus does not allow us to remain stagnant. He challenges us to rise to our highest potential. His presence accompanies us through the phases of stretching, shaping, and refining, ensuring that we evolve into our true selves. He perceives our latent capabilities, even when they are obscured to our own recognition.

To grow in alignment with the teachings of Jesus entails a commitment to trust in His processes. It involves surrendering to His guidance, with the understanding that the process of pruning serves as preparation for something far greater rather than as a form of punishment. The more one remains connected to Him, the more one is likely to thrive.

Genuine friendship encourages personal development. Jesus extends an invitation to engage in a transformative relationship that shapes character and enhances one's comprehension of love, grace, and truth. Through His gentle correction and inspirational teachings, individuals are empowered to relinquish outdated habits and to adopt a renewed existence in His illuminating presence. This journey of growth is both personal and communal, as His love radiates outward, influencing those in one's surrounding environment.

Reflections

- Are there areas in your life where God invites you to grow?
- How can you remain connected to Him and trust His process?

Prayer

Lord, thank You for inviting me to grow in Your image. Help me to embrace change and transformation, so that I may reflect Your glory in every aspect of my life.

"...If you remain in me and I in you, you will bear much fruit."

John 15:5

A Friend in Seasons of Success

"Commit to the Lord whatever you do, and He will establish your plans." — Proverbs 16:3 (NIV)

The audience erupted in applause as Solomon ascended to the throne. The young monarch had been selected to lead the people of God, following the legacy of his father, King David. The burden of leadership was substantial, yet the potential for success lay before him. He possessed access to wealth, power, and influence. However, prior to making any decisions, Solomon engaged in an unexpected course of action, he sought divine guidance.

On one occasion, God appeared to him in a dream and offered, "Request whatever you desire, and I shall grant it to you." Many rulers would have requested military strength, material wealth, or notoriety. In contrast, Solomon requested wisdom, recognizing that achievements devoid of divine counsel lack true fulfillment.

In times of prosperity, one can easily be tempted to rely solely on personal capabilities, overlooking the source of these blessings. It is essential to acknowledge that genuine success is derived from dedicating our endeavors to the Lord, seeking His wisdom, and understanding that all good things come from Him.

Success is not solely defined by the achievement of our pursuits; it also involves maintaining a connection to the source of our guidance. In both challenging and triumphant moments, support can be drawn from God. This guidance not only recognizes our accomplishments but also imparts lessons in humility and advocates for utilizing our successes to foster a positive impact on society.

Reflections

- How do you acknowledge Jesus' role in your successes?
- In what ways can you commit your plans to Him today?

Prayer

Jesus, thank You for walking with me in my moments of success. May I always remember that every blessing comes from You, and help me to use my achievements to honor Your name.

Our success
is for His
Glory.

A Friend Who Inspires Hope

"May the God of hope fill you with all joy and peace as you trust in him, so that you may overflow with hope by the power of the Holy Spirit." — Romans 15:13 (NIV)

Zacchaeus dedicated many years to accumulating wealth; however, this pursuit came at a significant cost, undermining his reputation, relationships, and internal peace. As a chief tax collector, he amassed riches by imposing excessive charges on his fellow citizens, which led to widespread disdain directed towards him. He was regarded as a traitor, a figure seemingly beyond the possibility of redemption.

However, upon hearing about Jesus, a figure renowned for healing the sick, forgiving transgressions, and embracing societal outcasts, Zacchaeus felt a glimmer of hope. He considered the possibility that this Jesus might perceive him in a different light.

There was a challenge, though: Zacchaeus was of short stature and could not see over the crowd of people. Nevertheless, he was resolute in his desire to see Jesus. He proactively ran ahead and climbed a sycamore tree, determined to catch a glimpse of Jesus as He proceeded through Jericho.

In an unexpected turn of events, Jesus halted His progress. He looked upward and met Zacchaeus' gaze. Contrary to the condemnation that Zacchaeus had anticipated from others, Jesus addressed him: "Zacchaeus, come down immediately. I must stay at your house today."

The crowd reacted with astonishment. Among all the individuals Jesus could have chosen to associate with, why did He select Zacchaeus? Did He not recognize the nature of the man in question?

However, Jesus possessed this understanding; He perceived more than Zacchaeus' past; He recognized his potential. In that pivotal moment, Zacchaeus experienced a transformation of heart. He warmly welcomed Jesus into his residence and, moved by the grace he received, proclaimed, "Behold, Lord! Here and now I shall give half of my possessions to the poor, and if I have defrauded anyone, I will repay fourfold."

Jesus inspired this change in Zacchaeus, not through condemnation but through love. He communicated to Zacchaeus that his story was not concluded, that he had the capacity to transcend his previous identity. Consequently, Zacchaeus emerged as a renewed individual.

In a similar manner, Jesus extends this same friendship to individuals today. He does not view us merely through the lens of our failures; rather, He perceives our potential for growth and transformation. He invites us to aspire to something greater, encouraging us to release the burdens of our past and embrace a life redefined by His love.

Jesus serves as a constant source of hope in a world frequently overshadowed by despair. His friendship enriches one's life with a hopeful outlook that surpasses existing circumstances. Even in times of uncertainty, His love reassures us that hope is enduring and that the promise of renewal follows every challenging moment. This hope serves as a sustaining force and motivates individuals to shine as beacons of light for others.

Reflections

- How does Jesus' love inspire you to see yourself and your future differently?
- In what ways can you share this hope with those who are struggling?

Prayer

Jesus, fill me with the hope that only You can provide. Let your light shine through me, inspiring others to see the promise and beauty ahead.

... my hope is
in you.

Psalms 39:7

A Friend Who Gives Us Peace

"Peace I leave with you; my peace I give you."
John 14:27 (NIV)

The conference room was filled with apprehensive murmurs. The participants understood that a significant change was imminent, one beyond their control. Jesus had articulated the notion of His impending departure, which weighed heavily on their hearts.

Subsequently, He gazed at them with compassion and stated, "Peace I leave with you; my peace I give you."

This peace was not akin to the superficial tranquility often offered by the world, temporary and fragile. Rather, it was profound and unshakeable, a peace that would endure even amid adversity.

Hours later, Jesus was apprehended, prompting them to disperse in trepidation. However, in the days that ensued, they would recall His words. When He later appeared to them, His initial greeting was, "Peace be with you."

The essence of Jesus' peace is not the mere absence of discord; rather, it embodies the assurance of His presence. In moments of profound turbulence, He reassures us with a quiet command, "Peace, be still."

Reflection

- What areas of your life do you need to surrender to Jesus' peace?

Prayer

Lord, thank You for being my rock and fortress. Help me to lean on Your strength and to rest in the security and peace that comes from knowing You are always by my side.

And the peace of God, which passeth all understanding, shall keep your hearts and minds through Christ Jesus.

Philippians 4:7

A Friend Who Inspires a Life of Gratitude

"Give thanks in all circumstances; for this is God's will for you in Christ Jesus." — 1 Thessalonians 5:18 (NIV)

Ten men stood at a distance, their expressions reflecting profound sorrow. They had been ostracized from their communities, compelled to reside on the periphery of society due to a debilitating disease. Leprosy had stripped them of their families, their dignity, and their hope. However, upon encountering Him, their circumstances began to shift.

"Jesus, Master, have mercy on us," they exclaimed fervently.

Jesus turned to them, His gaze imbued with compassion. Instead of distancing Himself, as was the common reaction. He issued instructions that would transform their lives: "Go, show yourselves to the priests."

Initially, no immediate change was observable. Nevertheless, as they proceeded in obedience to His command, their skin began to heal, their wounds vanished, and their physical forms were restored. They had experienced healing.

Overcome with elation, they hurried to the priests, eager to reclaim their previous lives. However, one individual paused. He turned back, his heart filled with gratitude. Falling at the feet of Jesus, he publicly praised God with great fervor.

Jesus observed His surroundings and remarked, "Were not ten cleansed? Where are the other nine?" He then turned to the one who expressed gratitude and stated, "Rise and go; your faith has made you well."

This passage from scripture serves as a profound reminder of the importance of gratitude in our lives. While the nine individuals received healing, only one returned to express appreciation, and in doing so, he received an even greater benefit. Gratitude transcends mere verbal acknowledgment; it involves a conscious recognition of the source of all blessings, ultimately pointing to a relational dynamic with the divine. His relentless love, guidance, and care encourage individuals to express gratitude for both the blessings and the lessons derived from life's challenges. Each day presents an opportunity to cultivate a mindset of thankfulness, thereby transforming routine experiences into meaningful celebrations of His grace and goodness.

Reflections

- What blessings, big or small, are you most grateful for today?
- How can you cultivate a heart of gratitude in every circumstance?

Prayer

Jesus, thank You for the abundant blessings in my life. Help me to embrace each day with a heart of gratitude, acknowledging Your presence in every situation.

I will bless
the Lord at
all times; His
praise shall
continually
be in my
mouth.

Psalms 34:1

A Friend Who Intercedes for Us

"He always lives to intercede for them."
Hebrews 7:25 (NIV)

Peter stood in the courtyard, attempting to warm his hands over the fire, while, inside, Jesus faced a trial characterized by accusations and physical abuse.

Hours prior, Peter had asserted his unwavering loyalty, declaring, "Even if I have to die with you, I will never disown you."

However, as fear took hold of him, a servant girl identified him, stating, "You were with Jesus."

Peter denied it, responding, "I do not know Him."

This denial occurred a second time and then a third. Following this, the rooster crowed, and at that moment, Peter experienced a profound sense of failure.

Nevertheless, prior to this incident, Jesus had imparted words of encouragement: "Simon, Satan has requested to sift all of you like wheat. However, I have prayed for you, Simon, that your faith may not fail." (Luke 22:31-32)

Before Peter experienced his failure, Jesus was already interceding on his behalf. This intercession extends to all individuals as He stands before the Father, advocating for us and enfolding us in grace. In moments of our shortcomings, He refrains from condemnation; rather, He continues to intercede for us.

Reflection

- How does knowing Jesus prays for you change how you see your struggles?

Prayer

Dear Lord, thank you for your unwavering presence as my intercessor. Even when I have strayed from your path, you have consistently stood by me, advocating for my heart. Your compassion knows no bounds, and I am deeply grateful for your gentle guidance. Help me to embrace that same spirit of intercession for others, teaching me to offer love and support as you have shown to me.

He
intercedes
on our
behalf
covering us
with grace
for each
day.

A Friend Who Calls Us to More

"Come, follow me." Matthew 4:19 (NIV)

The fishing nets felt heavy in Simon's hands, dampened by the morning's labor. His entire existence had revolved around this life on the water, characterized by the processes of casting and gathering.

Then, an unexpected voice disrupted his routine.

"Come, follow me, and I will make you fishers of men."

At this juncture, Simon, who would later be known as Peter, confronted a pivotal decision: remain within the confines of the familiar or venture into the unknown.

He chose to relinquish the nets.

This narrative illustrates how Jesus invites individuals to transcend their current circumstances and comfort zones, guiding them toward a life imbued with purpose. He perceives potential in individuals that they may not recognize in themselves. While His call may seem illogical at times, the outcome is invariably rewarding.

Jesus embodies not only the role of a comforting friend but also that of a mentor who challenges individuals to pursue personal growth.

Reflections

- Is there an area where Jesus is calling you to step out in faith?
- What is holding you back?

Prayer

Today, I embrace the call to step into your path and experience greater things through you. I recognize that by trusting you fully, I will find alignment.

He is able to do exceedingly abundantly above all we ask or think

Ephesians 3:20

A Friend Who Will Return for Us

*"And if I go and prepare a place for you, I
will come back and take you to be with me."*
John 14:3 (NIV)

The disciples gathered around Jesus, burdened by the prospect of His imminent departure. They had accompanied Him for several years; it was difficult to envision continuing without His presence.

In response, He articulated a promise that would provide them with sustenance through each challenge they would encounter: "Do not let your hearts be troubled; I will return and take you to be with me."

Although centuries have elapsed since those words were spoken, the promise remains intact. He is indeed coming again.

Jesus is a steadfast friend who does not forsake us. He is in the process of preparing a place for us, a sanctuary where sorrow and suffering will cease to exist. Although the period of waiting may seem prolonged, the day will inevitably arrive when we will behold Him face-to-face.

Upon that moment's arrival, we will recognize that every effort and sacrifice was worthwhile.

Reflection

- How does the promise of Jesus' return shape how you live today?

Prayer

Thank you, Lord, for your promise of a home with you. With joyful expectation, I await the day You will return, and that promise will be fulfilled.

His promises are true.

About the Author

Nedra Reid is a life and grief coach, faith-filled storyteller, and passionate voice of hope for those navigating life's deepest valleys and most sacred joys. As the author of Friend: A 31-Day Devotional on Jesus as a Friend to Humanity, Nedra invites readers into a journey that unveils the tender, unwavering friendship of Christ in every season of life.

Her work is deeply rooted in her calling to walk alongside others through loss, healing, and renewal. She is the author of *Grief Mode*, a guided journal designed to empower hearts to process pain, embrace purpose, and rediscover peace through faith. She is also a contributing author in the inspirational anthology *Becoming an Unstoppable Woman in Faith*, where her story continues to impact lives around the world.

Nedra's mission is to help others encounter the healing presence of God in real, tangible ways.

For more resources, devotionals, and encouragement, visit www.thereider.com.

www.ingramcontent.com/pod-product-compliance
Lightning Source LLC
Chambersburg PA
CBHW051637120626
46551CB00014B/2114